Step 1
Go to **www.openlightbox.com**

Step 2
Enter this unique code
RCHNDBA96

Step 3
Explore your interactive eBook!

Your interactive eBook comes with...

Australian Shepherd
Start!
Share

AV2 is optimized for use on any device

 Read

 Audio Listen to the entire book read aloud

 Videos Watch informative video clips

 Weblinks Gain additional information for research

 Try This! Complete activities and hands-on experiments

  Key Words Study vocabulary, and complete a matching word activity

 Quizzes Test your knowledge

 Slideshows View images and captions

 Share Share titles within your Learning Management System (LMS) or Library Circulation System

 Citation Create bibliographical references following APA, CMOS, and MLA styles

This title is part of our AV2 digital subscription

1-Year K–2 Subscription
ISBN 978-1-7911-3310-8

Access hundreds of AV2 titles with our digital subscription.
Sign up for a FREE trial at **www.openlightbox.com/trial**

The digital components of this book are guaranteed to stay active for at least five years from the date of publication.

Australian Shepherd

CONTENTS

- 2 Interactive eBook Code
- 4 Smart and Active
- 6 Medium-Sized Dogs
- 8 Coat Colors
- 10 Growing Up
- 12 Herding Dogs
- 14 Exercise
- 16 Grooming
- 18 Food and Attention
- 20 Staying Healthy
- 22 Incredible Australian Shepherds
- 24 Sight Words

My Australian shepherd is a smart dog.

He is very alert and likes to stay active.

Australian shepherds are medium in size. They are quick and athletic.

Dog Shoulder Heights

Border Collie
Up to 22 inches
(56 centimeters)

Australian Shepherd
Up to 23 inches
(58 cm)

Great Pyrenees
Up to 32 inches
(81 cm)

My Australian shepherd has a patterned coat of fur. It is called a red merle coat.

Australian shepherds can also be blue merle, red, or black.

Many Australian shepherd puppies are born with bright blue eyes.

The color of their eyes may change as they grow up.

Where in the World

While they are named after Australia, Australian shepherds actually come from the United States.

Australian shepherds make good herding dogs.

Some are trained to guide sheep and cattle for farmers.

My Australian shepherd needs more exercise than most dogs.

We go on long runs every day.

He also needs to exercise his mind. I give him dog puzzles and teach him tricks.

My Australian shepherd has a thick coat.

I brush him often. This keeps his fur clean and free of tangles.

I also spend plenty of time with him. We practice tricks together.

I take my Australian shepherd to the veterinarian at least once a year.

The veterinarian helps keep my dog healthy.

Dog Breed Popularity in the United States

#11

Pembroke Welsh Corgi

#12

Australian Shepherd

#13

Yorkshire Terrier

Incredible Australian Shepherds

In the **late 1800s**, Australian shepherds were bred to help **cowboys** and **ranchers** in the western United States.

Some Australian shepherds have **one blue eye** and **one brown eye**.

Australian shepherds have a **strong herding instinct**. They may try to herd children and other pets.

Many Australian shepherds compete in dog sports, such as **agility contests** and **herding trials**.

SIGHT WORDS

Research has shown that as much as 65 percent of all written material published in English is made up of 300 words. These 300 words cannot be taught using pictures or learned by sounding them out. They must be recognized by sight. This book contains 65 common sight words to help young readers improve their reading fluency and comprehension. This book also teaches young readers several important content words, such as proper nouns. These words are paired with pictures to aid in learning and improve understanding.

Page	Sight Words First Appearance
4	a, and, he, is, likes, my, to, very
6	are, great, in, they, up
9	also, be, can, has, it, of, or
10	eyes, many, with
11	after, as, change, come, from, grow, may, states, the, their, where, while, world
12	for, good, make, some
14	day, every, go, long, more, most, needs, on, runs, than, we
15	give, him, his, I
17	keeps, often, this
19	time, together
20	at, helps, once, take, year

Page	Content Words First Appearance
4	Australian shepherd, dog
6	border collie, great Pyrenees, heights, shoulder, size
9	coat, fur
10	puppies
11	Australia, color, United States
12	cattle, farmers, sheep
14	exercise
15	mind, puzzles, tricks
17	fur, tangles
20	breed, Pembroke Welsh corgi, popularity, veterinarian, Yorkshire terrier

Published by Lightbox Learning Inc.
276 5th Avenue, Suite 704 #917
New York, NY 10001
Website: www.openlightbox.com

Copyright ©2026 Lightbox Learning Inc.
All rights reserved. No part of this publication may be reproduced, stored in a retrieval system, or transmitted in any form or by any means, electronic, mechanical, photocopying, recording, or otherwise, without the prior written permission of the publisher.

Library of Congress Control Number: 2024057491

ISBN 979-8-8745-2143-1 (hardcover)
ISBN 979-8-8745-2144-8 (softcover)
ISBN 979-8-8745-2145-5 (static multi-user eBook)
ISBN 979-8-8745-2147-9 (interactive multi-user eBook)

012025
100924

Printed in Guangzhou, China
1 2 3 4 5 6 7 8 9 0 29 28 27 26 25

Project Coordinator: Priyanka Das
Designer: Jean Faye Rodriguez

Every reasonable effort has been made to trace ownership and to obtain permission to reprint copyright material. The publisher would be pleased to have any errors or omissions brought to its attention so that they may be corrected in subsequent printings.

The publisher acknowledges Getty Images and Shutterstock as its primary image suppliers for this title.